Inside the NHL

Edmonton Oilers

Erin Butler

AV² provides enriched content that supplements and complements this book. Weigl's AV² books strive to create inspired learning and engage young minds in a total learning experience.

Your AV² Media Enhanced books come alive with...

Audio
Listen to sections of the book read aloud.

Key Words
Study vocabulary, and complete a matching word activity.

Go to **www.av2books.com,** and enter this book's unique code.

Video
Watch informative video clips.

Quizzes
Test your knowledge.

BOOK CODE

I 6 5 6 9 8 6

Embedded Weblinks
Gain additional information for research.

Slide Show
View images and captions, and prepare a presentation.

AV² by Weigl brings you media enhanced books that support active learning.

Try This!
Complete activities and hands-on experiments.

... and much, much more!

Published by AV² by Weigl
350 5th Avenue, 59th Floor
New York, NY 10118
Websites: www.av2books.com   www.weigl.com

Library of Congress Control Number: 2014951971

ISBN 978-1-4896-3140-4 (hardcover)
ISBN 978-1-4896-4015-4 (softcover)
ISBN 978-1-4896-3141-1 (single-user eBook)
ISBN 978-1-4896-3142-8 (multi-user eBook)

Printed in the United States of America in Brainerd, Minnesota
1 2 3 4 5 6 7 8 9 0 19 18 17 16 15

032015
WEP050315

Senior Editor Heather Kissock
Art Director Terry Paulhus

Photo Credits
Every reasonable effort has been made to trace ownership and to obtain permission to reprint copyright material. The publishers would be pleased to have any errors or omissions brought to their attention so that they may be corrected in subsequent printings.

Weigl acknowledges Getty Images and iStock as its primary image suppliers for this title.

Edmonton Oilers

CONTENTS

Introduction

The Edmonton Oilers have seen the best and worst that the National Hockey League (NHL) has to offer. After becoming a part of the NHL when the league merged with the **World Hockey Association (WHA)**, the Oilers leaped to lofty status as an NHL superpower. Behind the play of stars such as "The Great One," Wayne Gretzky, the Oilers won five Stanley Cup championships between 1983 and 1990.

Oilers fans hope talented young players like Taylor Hall will help the team accomplish their quest for a sixth Stanley Cup.

Facing financial troubles in the late 1980s, Oilers management began trading away core players, including Gretzky. The ripples from the multiple trades gradually took effect, and the Oilers were suddenly among the worst teams in the NHL. Edmonton is a proud hockey community that has been to the top of the mountain. In recent years, the Oilers have built up a talented young roster and are ready to climb that mountain again.

Even non-hockey fans can identify Gretzky as one of hockey's all-time greats.

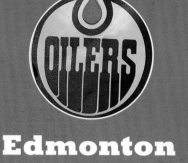

Edmonton OILERS

Arena Rexall Place

Division Pacific

Head Coach Todd Nelson

Location Edmonton, Alberta, Canada

NHL Stanley Cup Titles 1984, 1985, 1987, 1988, 1990

Nicknames The Oil

5 Stanley Cup Titles

7 Retired Numbers

20 Playoff Appearances

6 Division Titles

History

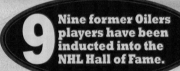

9 Nine former Oilers players have been inducted into the NHL Hall of Fame.

Gretzky is the only player in NHL history to record a 200-point season. He did it four times during his 10 seasons with the Oilers.

The Oilers began play in 1972 as the Alberta Oilers of the WHA. The next year, they changed their name to the Edmonton Oilers. When the WHA merged with the NHL in 1979, the Oilers entered a new era in a new league. Luckily for them, they entered this new era with arguably the greatest player in NHL history—Wayne Gretzky.

Along with other **All-Star** players such as Mark Messier, Jari Kurri, Paul Coffey, and Grant Fuhr, Gretzky led the Oilers to the top of the league during a dominant eight-year stretch. The 1983 to 1990 team reached the status of a dynasty, and the Oilers collected records and awards both as individuals and as a team. They won a remarkable five Stanley Cup titles in eight years.

When financial troubles hit the team in the late 1980s, management was forced to make the tough decision to trade The Great One. Gretzky's trade to the Los Angeles Kings was the most shocking trade in NHL history. Today, the Oilers are focused on building a team of talented young offensive players, hoping to use the same formula they used in winning five Cups.

During the 1989–1990 season, Mark Messier led the Oilers to their fifth Stanley Cup title, and their first without Gretzky.

The Arena

With less than 17,000 seats, Rexall Place is a cozy arena without a bad seat in the house.

The Oilers' arena has undergone a number of changes through the years, most of which have altered the actual name of the arena. First, it was known as the Northlands Coliseum. It was then known as the Skyreach Centre, and finally became Rexall Place in 2003, when the Rexall drugstore company bought its **naming rights**.

For an NHL arena, Rexall Place is small. During the regular season, it is a notoriously quiet arena as fans pay careful attention to the game. When the **playoffs** roll around though, a once quiet arena becomes a loud and intimidating place to play. One of the most appreciated features of the arena, at least by the players, is the newly renovated, state-of-the-art dressing rooms for both the Oilers and their opponents. In addition to the facilities it offers, the arena also displays five replicas of the team's Stanley Cups, with symbolic space left for a sixth trophy.

The ownership of the Oilers recently announced that it would be building a new arena called Rogers Place. It is set to open in 2016. The new, and bigger, arena will be ready to support a rising team.

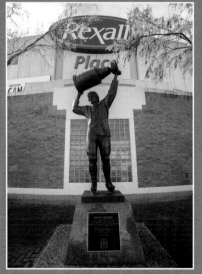

A statue of hockey legend Wayne Gretzky stands tall outside of Rexall Place.

Where They Play

British Columbia

Alberta

CANADA

Saskatchewan

Manitoba

Ontario

7

3

14

★**4** Rexall Place, Edmonton

Washington

Montana

North Dakota

Minnesota

Wisconsin

11

8

Oregon

Idaho

South Dakota

Iowa

Wyoming

Nebraska

Illinois

6

Nevada

Utah

Colorado

Kansas

Missouri

UNITED STATES

13

California

9

5

1

Arizona

New Mexico

Oklahoma

Arkansas

2

Texas

Louisiana

10

Mis

Pacific Ocean

MEXICO

Gulf of Mexico

WESTERN CONFERENCE

PACIFIC DIVISION

1 Anaheim Ducks
2 Arizona Coyotes
3 Calgary Flames
★4 Edmonton Oilers
5 Los Angeles Kings
6 San Jose Sharks
7 Vancouver Canucks

CENTRAL DIVISION

8 Chicago Blackhawks
9 Colorado Avalanche
10 Dallas Stars
11 Minnesota Wild
12 Nashville Predators
13 St. Louis Blues
14 Winnipeg Jets

Newfoundland

Quebec

Prince Edward Island

New Brunswick

New Hampshire

Vermont

Maine

20

Nova Scotia

19

15

Massachusetts

22

26

Rhode Island

27

New York

Connecticut

17

25

16

New Jersey

Michigan

Pennsylvania

29

28

Ohio

Delaware

Indiana

30

Maryland

24

West Virginia

Virginia

District of Columbia

Kentucky

23

North Carolina

Tennessee

12

South Carolina

Alabama

Georgia

sippi

Atlantic Ocean

Florida

21

18

Rexall Place

Arena
Rexall Place

Location
7424 118th Avenue
Edmonton, Alberta T5B 4M9

Broke Ground
November 3, 1972

Completed
November 30, 1974

Features
- statue of Wayne Gretzky
- renovated dressing rooms
- five Stanley Cup replicas

LEGEND
☆ Rexall Place
▪ Eastern Conference
▪ Western Conference

ATLANTIC DIVISION

15 Boston Bruins	19 Montreal Canadiens
16 Buffalo Sabres	20 Ottawa Senators
17 Detroit Red Wings	21 Tampa Bay Lightning
18 Florida Panthers	22 Toronto Maple Leafs

METROPOLITAN DIVISION

23 Carolina Hurricanes	27 New York Rangers
24 Columbus Blue Jackets	28 Philadelphia Flyers
25 New Jersey Devils	29 Pittsburgh Penguins
26 New York Islanders	30 Washington Capitals

The Uniforms

The Oilers have retired **SEVEN** jerseys.

The Oilers brought back their bright orange uniform in 2008, after retiring it for the previous 11 seasons.

HOME

Since their founding in the WHA, the Oilers have made only slight changes to their uniforms. The uniforms highlight the team's colors of blue, orange, and white, although there was a period when they used midnight blue, red, and bronze. Today, the home jersey is mainly blue with orange and white accents. The away jersey is mainly white with blue and orange accents.

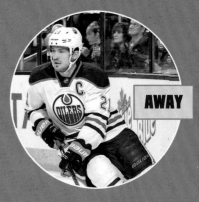

AWAY

On the front of the jersey is the team **logo**. The logo pays tribute to Edmonton's status as the head of Canada's oil industry, which also gave the team its name. It features a drop of oil over the word "Oilers."

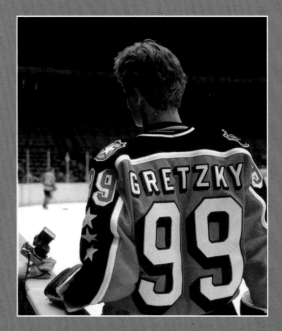

Wayne Gretzky's number 99 was not only retired by the Oilers, it was retired league-wide by the NHL in 2000.

Helmets and Face Masks

Oilers helmets began to feature a player's **NUMBER** on them during the 2011–2012 season.

The overall use of visors during the 2013–2014 NHL season was 77.8 percent. Oiler Taylor Hall is among the group of current players who has opted for the visor and more facial protection.

Like all NHL teams, the Oilers use different helmets for home and away games. Their helmets match their team colors. For home games, they use a blue helmet, and for away games, a white one. The helmet features the team logo on the side. That logo is a blue circle with an orange oil drop hanging from the top of it. Underneath, in letters that look like they are dripping oil, is the word "Oilers."

Goaltenders for the Oilers have chosen unique face masks over the years. One of the most memorable was Grant Fuhr's mask, which featured the Oilers' logo, but in a bold and striking way. More recently, goaltender Viktor Fasth upgraded from a blank mask to a new one that displays gears, highlighting Edmonton's industrial past. Many Oilers goaltenders have highlighted industry and fearlessness as themes for their masks.

Oilers goalies take elements of the city of Edmonton, as well as the team logo and colors, and design helmets that are as much about art as they are safety.

The Coaches

3 Three former Oilers NHL players returned to the team as head coach.

Coaching is never an easy job, but a roster full of All-Stars in the 1980s certainly helped out Glen Sather.

In the early days, Oilers' coaches had a fairly easy time earning victories. This was because they were overseeing a group of talented young players who were all reaching the prime of their careers at the same time. The coaches had the exciting job of mixing and matching that talent. More recently, consistent victories and sustained success have been harder to come by.

GLEN SATHER A former NHL player, Glen Sather became head coach for the WHA Oilers in 1976. He was partially responsible for signing Gretzky as well as star players such as Mark Messier. This began the Oilers' remarkable run in the 1980s. Sather, who was with the team until 1989, has since been inducted into the Hall of Fame.

CRAIG MACTAVISH Another former Oilers player, Craig MacTavish, was a talented coach who won more than 300 games in his career. He led the Oilers to the Stanley Cup Final in 2006, the team's first Cup appearance since 1990. Today, he is the general manager of the Oilers.

TODD NELSON Nelson came on board after the Oilers were only able to post seven victories in the team's first 30 games of the 2014–2015 season. Nelson, who was coaching the Oilers' minor league team in Oklahoma City at the time of his hiring, will move behind an NHL bench for the first time as the head man for the Oilers. After eight straight playoff-less seasons, Nelson has a clear objective, return the once proud **franchise** to the postseason.

Fans and the Internet

Oilers fans are some of the most enthusiastic in all of the NHL, often showing up to games dressed in head-to-toe team gear.

The Oilers have the difficult job of creating and maintaining a fan base in the rather remote city of Edmonton. The team has not won a championship since 1990, and many of their youngest fans have yet to experience the Oilers raising a Stanley Cup. Still, due to the franchise's early and sustained success—and the passionate hockey culture in Edmonton—the team has built up an enormous fan base.

Oilers fans are very active on the internet. For news, they visit popular websites such as Copper & Blue, OilFans.com, and Oilers Nation. They also connect with each other on the official Oilers message board and on blogs such as Oilogosphere. The team also supports programs for their fans, including Fan Zone and Kids Club.

Signs
of a fan

#1 The Oilers produce *Oil Country Magazine* so that fans can keep up with the latest and greatest news about their team.

#2 A recent addition to the team's in-game entertainment is a group of cheerleaders called the Oilers Octane, who have been supporting the team since the 2010–2011 season.

Legends of the Past

Many great players have suited up for the Oilers. A few of them have become icons of the team and the city it represents.

Position: Center
NHL Seasons: 20 (1979–1999)
Born: January 26, 1961, in Brantford, Ontario, Canada

Wayne Gretzky

Known as "The Great One," Wayne Gretzky is arguably the best hockey player the world has ever seen. After beginning his career with the Indianapolis Racers, he went to the Edmonton Oilers, where he played until 1988. While leading the Oilers to four Stanley Cup titles, Gretzky demolished numerous NHL records along the way. Perhaps most notably, he scored 92 goals in a single season. Gretzky also became the first NHL player to record more than 200 points in a single season. He accomplished that feat four times. In 1999, he was inducted into the Hall of Fame.

Mark Messier

As a teammate and friend of Gretzky, Mark Messier was another key part of the Oilers dynasty of the 1980s. Large in size and fearless on the ice, Messier was not only a great offensive player, but also was a skilled defender. He was particularly praised for his leadership skills. In fact, he became the first player to lead two different teams to Stanley Cup titles as a captain. Messier ranks second in all-time NHL points and third in **assists**. He won six Stanley Cup titles and has been inducted into the Hall of Fame.

Position: Center
NHL Seasons: 25 (1979–2004)
Born: January 18, 1961, in Edmonton, Alberta, Canada

Jari Kurri

Jari Kurri was another star member of the Oilers' dynasty during the 1980s, playing right wing on a **line** with Gretzky. Although he quietly went about his business and was often overlooked, Kurri was an offensive powerhouse in his own right. He recorded more than 600 goals in his NHL career. Kurri led European-born NHL players in goals, assists, and points during that time, while also representing his native Finland in international competitions. Kurri is a member of the NHL Hall of Fame.

Position: Right Wing
NHL Seasons: 18 (1980–1998)
Born: May 18, 1960, in Helsinki, Finland

Grant Fuhr

Rounding out the powerhouse Oilers team of the 1980s was goaltender Grant Fuhr. His phenomenal goalkeeping fit right in with the skilled offense and defense of the Oilers, helping to guide the Oilers to five Stanley Cup titles. During his career, Fuhr won the Vezina Trophy as the league's best goaltender and the William M. Jennings Trophy for having the fewest **goals against average**. After being traded from the Oilers, Fuhr continued his success, racking up more than 400 career wins. He was inducted into the Hall of Fame in 2003.

Position: Goaltender
NHL Seasons: 19 (1981–2000)
Born: September 28, 1962, in Spruce Grove, Alberta, Canada

Stars of Today

T oday's Oilers team is made up of many young, talented players who have proven that they are among the best in the league.

Taylor Hall

T aylor Hall is one of the most exciting prospects for the current Oilers team. He has played for the Oilers since beginning his NHL career in 2010 and has steadily improved. Along with having fantastic skating skills, Hall has quickly established himself as one of the top scorers on the team. He has recorded three career **hat tricks** and set a team record for the shortest time to score two goals, which he accomplished in just eight seconds. As he enters the prime of his career, Hall hopes to lead the Oilers into another era of sustained success.

Position: Left Wing
NHL Seasons: 4 (2010–Present)
Born: November 14, 1991, in Calgary, Alberta, Canada

Jordan Eberle

J ordan Eberle joined the Oilers at about the same time as teammate Taylor Hall, and together, they have been dominant scorers for the team. Eberle is a consistent, hardworking player who is depended on to log substantial minutes on the ice. He has tallied more than 200 points in his NHL career, and had 20 multi-point games in both the 2011–2012 and the 2013–2014 seasons. With his tendency to shoot the puck with accuracy, Eberle is another bright spot for this proud franchise.

Position: Right Wing
NHL Seasons: 4 (2010–Present)
Born: May 15, 1990, in Regina, Saskatchewan, Canada

Ryan Nugent-Hopkins

The young center for the Oilers, Ryan Nugent-Hopkins joined the team in 2011. Nugent-Hopkins is considered to be the engine that makes the Oilers go. Although still a very young player, he has great patience with the puck, and displays unique leadership qualities. A true playmaker, Nugent-Hopkins is a skilled passer, who often sets up his wingers for easy goals and makes his teammates better. As a **rookie**, Nugent-Hopkins recorded his first career hat trick and was a finalist for the Calder Memorial Trophy for rookie of the year.

Position: Center
NHL Seasons: 3 (2011–Present)
Born: April 12, 1993, in Burnaby, British Columbia, Canada

All-Time Records

1,037
Most Games Played
As a player, Kevin Lowe set a record for the most games played for the Oilers.

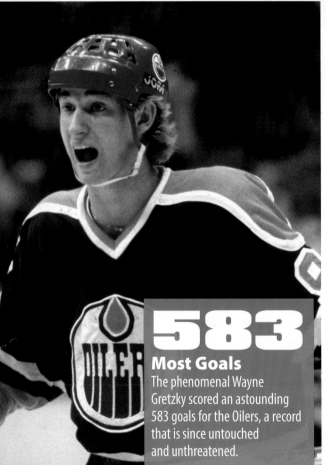

1,086
Most Assists
Gretzky also leads the team in assists, and his lead is a commanding one. Gretzky has 400 more assists than another Oilers' great, Mark Messier, who is second on this list.

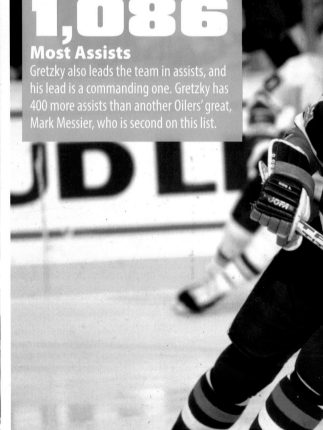

583
Most Goals
The phenomenal Wayne Gretzky scored an astounding 583 goals for the Oilers, a record that is since untouched and unthreatened.

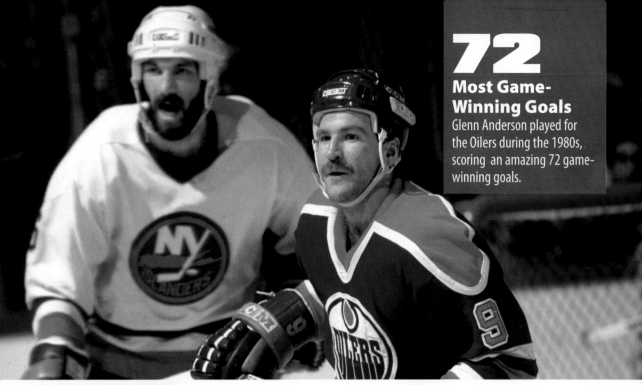

72
Most Game-Winning Goals
Glenn Anderson played for the Oilers during the 1980s, scoring an amazing 72 game-winning goals.

226
Most Wins as Goaltender
During the magic of the Oilers ruling era, Grant Fuhr posted a team record for wins as a goalie.

Timeline

Throughout the team's history, the Edmonton Oilers have had many memorable events that have become defining moments for the team and its fans.

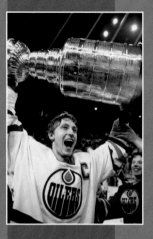

1978
The Oilers buy Wayne Gretzky's contract from the failing Indianapolis Racers. This acquisition proves to be the most meaningful in franchise history.

1984
The Oilers win their first Stanley Cup title, winning in five games against the defending champion New York Islanders.

| 1978 | 1980 | | 1982 | 1984 | 1986 | 1988 |

During the WHA-NHL merger, the Oilers become part of the NHL. They add more stars to their lineup to complement Gretzky.

1988
With a sweep against the Boston Bruins, the Oilers win their fourth Stanley Cup. Gretzky wins the Conn Smythe Trophy, as the Most Valuable Player (MVP) of the playoffs, for the second time.

1982
Wayne Gretzky scores his 77th goal, setting a new NHL record for most goals in a season. He would go on to score 92 goals during the 1981–1982 season.

The Future

Since the mainstays of the 1980s teams departed, the Oilers have seen their fair share of struggles. They have been forced to build from the ground up, hoping to reestablish themselves as an elite franchise. With a recent coaching change, and a talented and youthful roster, the future is once again looking bright.

1990

The Oilers win their fifth Stanley Cup title against the Boston Bruins, this time without Gretzky, who was traded two years prior. They defeat the Boston Bruins in five games.

Things are looking up for the Oilers in 2006 as they reach the Stanley Cup Final. They lose to the Carolina Hurricanes in seven games.

| 1990 | 1995 | 2000 | 2005 | 2010 | 2015 |

1999

On opening night, the Oilers retire Gretzky's famous number 99 jersey.

1993

With most of their finest players now long gone, the Oilers begin to suffer. For the first time since entering the NHL, the team fails to make the playoffs.

2014

Todd Nelson is named head coach of the Oilers.

Write a Biography

Life Story

A person's life story can be the subject of a book. This kind of book is called a biography. Biographies often describe the lives of people who have achieved great success. These people may be alive today, or they may have lived many years ago. Reading a biography can help you learn more about a great person.

Get the Facts

Use this book, and research in the library and on the internet, to find out more about your favorite Oiler. Learn as much about this player as you can. What position does he play? What are his statistics in important categories? Has he set any records? Also, be sure to write down key events in the person's life. What was his childhood like? What has he accomplished off the field? Is there anything else that makes this person special or unusual?

Use the Concept Web

A concept web is a useful research tool. Read the questions in the concept web on the following page. Answer the questions in your notebook. Your answers will help you write a biography.

Concept Web

Adulthood
- Where does this individual currently reside?
- Does he or she have a family?

Your Opinion
- What did you learn from the books you read in your research?
- Would you suggest these books to others?
- Was anything missing from these books?

Childhood
- Where and when was this person born?
- Describe his or her parents, siblings, and friends.
- Did this person grow up in unusual circumstances?

Accomplishments off the Field
- What is this person's life's work?
- Has he or she received awards or recognition for accomplishments?
- How have this person's accomplishments served others?

Write a Biography

Help and Obstacles
- Did this individual have a positive attitude?
- Did he or she receive help from others?
- Did this person have a mentor?
- Did this person face any hardships?
- If so, how were the hardships overcome?

Accomplishments on the Field
- What records does this person hold?
- What key games and plays have defined his career?
- What are his stats in categories important to his position?

Work and Preparation
- What was this person's education?
- What was his or her work experience?
- How does this person work?
- What is the process he or she uses?

Trivia Time

Take this quiz to test your knowledge of the Edmonton Oilers. The answers are printed upside down under each question.

1 In what league did the Oilers play in before joining the NHL?

A. World Hockey Association (WHA)

2 How many Stanley Cup titles have the Oilers won?

A. Five

3 How many Stanley Cups have the Oilers won without Wayne Gretzky?

A. One

4 What is the name of the Oilers' arena?

A. Rexall Place

5 What is the name of the Oilers' head coach?

A. Todd Nelson

6 What will the new arena for the Oilers be called?

A. Rogers Place

7 What are the Oilers' team colors?

A. Orange, blue, and white

8 What color is the drop of oil on the team's logo?

A. Orange

9 Who served as head coach for the Oilers during their championship run in the 1980s?

A. Glen Sather

Key Words

All-Star: a game made for the best-ranked players in the NHL that happens mid-season. A player can be named an All-Star and then be sent to play in this game.

assists: a statistic that is attributed to up to two players of the scoring team who shoot, pass, or deflect the puck toward the scoring teammate

franchise: a team that is a member of a professional sports league

goals against average: a statistic that is the average of goals allowed per game by a goaltender

hat tricks: when a player scores three goals in one game

line: forwards who play in a group, or "shift," during a game

logo: a symbol that stands for a team or organization

naming rights: a form of advertisement for a company or another business that pays to have its name advertised at the forefront of an NHL arena

playoffs: a series of games that occur after regular season play

rookie: a player age 26 or younger who has played no more than 25 games in a previous season, nor six or more games in two previous seasons

World Hockey Association (WHA): the North American professional hockey league that merged with the NHL in 1979

Index

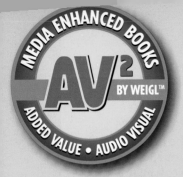

Log on to www.av2books.com

AV² by Weigl brings you media enhanced books that support active learning. Go to www.av2books.com, and enter the special code found on page 2 of this book. You will gain access to enriched and enhanced content that supplements and complements this book. Content includes video, audio, weblinks, quizzes, a slide show, and activities.

AV² Online Navigation

Book Pages
AV² pages directly correspond to pages in the book.

Audio
Listen to sections of the book read aloud.

Video
Watch informative video clips.

Embedded Weblinks
Gain additional information for research.

Key Words
Study vocabulary, and complete a matching word activity.

Quizzes
Test your knowledge.

Slide Show
View images and captions, and prepare a presentation.

Try This!
Complete activities and hands-on experiments.

AV² was built to bridge the gap between print and digital. We encourage you to tell us what you like and what you want to see in the future.

Sign up to be an AV² Ambassador at www.av2books.com/ambassador.

Due to the dynamic nature of the Internet, some of the URLs and activities provided as part of AV² by Weigl may have changed or ceased to exist. AV² by Weigl accepts no responsibility for any such changes. All media enhanced books are regularly monitored to update addresses and sites in a timely manner. Contact AV² by Weigl at 1-866-649-3445 or av2books@weigl.com with any questions, comments, or feedback.